I0503563

The S.K.I.E. Initiative

Table of Contents

Preface

What makes a good leader? I am sure this question has been asked by people in all sorts of positions and circumstances, in varying industries and organizations, from those in leadership to those who aspire to be in one eventually. And, as with any idea that involves us as humans, it is subjective. We all possess an idea of what we believe to be an ideal leader. Some say a leader is a teacher or a guide; others may say that they need to be bold, confident; while others may say they need to be understanding and steadfast. In truth, it is my belief that a leader is all of the above and more. And that is why I wrote this book.

If you go online and search, you can literally come across hundreds and hundreds of articles, blogs, books, and literature on how to be a great leader, or the blue print of awesome leadership, or something about the Top 10 characteristics of an ideal leader. Now they may be accurate, or they could be absolute nonsense; I have no idea, I haven't read them all. But what I do know is what my experience in my career in emergency services and as a leader in various industries and organizations has taught me and what I've learned from all the wonderful people I have had the honor of working and serving with.

The purpose of this book is not to introduce some new fangled step-by-step-make-you-the-best-leader-of-the-world process or some spaced-out theory on how to obtain pure harmony within your team. This is about working with real people with real issues and unique and individual ideas, histories, perceptions, and identities. It is about helping find yourself and your position in your own life and how to use those strengths (and weaknesses) to motivate, challenge, and empower your team to reach their goals and beyond, whether you are in a position of leadership or not.

I was inspired to write this book not only by my own experiences, but also by those individuals whom I've worked with or partnered with and discovering that there is a desire and need by people to have not only qualified people as leaders, but genuine people overall. People who understand the purpose of the team and what the individual members of the team need in order to help the team fulfill its purpose.

I was also inspired by the continuing changes and challenges facing people managers and team leaders today. There are so many factors that can influence our people as individuals and as a team. As leaders, part of our mission and drive is to find ways to ensure we are reaching and actively engaging our teammates and making sure we are having a positive impact on them.

Before we start with all that, I want to thank God for this life we have and for the opportunity to share all that I've learned so far and through whom all things are possible.

Also, a very special thanks to all those who have inspired me (you know who you are), especially my wonderful wife Jasmin, whom without I would not have the courage, desire, and inspiration to even attempt such an endeavor.

And a very, very special thank you to all who are reading. I hope that you find inspiration, motivation, or anything that can help you in either your work or personal life. I hope you enjoy.

Introduction

The SKIE Leadership initiative is based on four actions I believe every leader should engage in before developing a team, taking a leadership position, or before engaging in a new project. They are:

Self-Analyze

Know

Invest

Empower

These are basic concepts that should be the base of active leadership. In the following chapters, we will review these actions and ideas and how they serve to strengthen your leadership foundation and how they can impact your team as a whole and individually.

I developed this program after years of managing and working with people, developing teams, and after quite a few failures and hard times. It is not a perfect system, but one of the core ideas that helped me understand true leadership is the realization and acceptance that people are not perfect, and that being imperfect is absolutely, 100% OK. Much like a jigsaw puzzle, we must understand and accept that within our teams there are various pieces with their uneven and unique edges and find a way to place them together in order to complete the picture.

The integral concept to keep in mind with the SKIE Initiative is that it encourages you to operate within your team, and yourself, with integrity, honesty, and transparency. The idea is to not only get the best out of your team, but the best out of yourself for your team.

Chapter 1: Self-Analyze

"There are three things extremely hard: steel, a diamond, and to know one's self."
– Benjamin Franklin

They say that every journey begins with a first step. While this is true, I believe there is something that one must do before taking that first step, and that is to know where you are to begin with. I find myself chatting with people who have a desire to progress in their career or in life and have a tough time moving forward, and many times it because they don't take the time to see where they are or the varying directions they can move in.

In terms of being in a position of leadership, it is important for us to know where we stand, or what I call our personal position, not only in our career but also as a person overall. Not only because we will have the responsibility of leading a group of people, but along with that we will be a source of guidance, information, and direction for that group, and if we are uncertain of our personal position, or ourselves, then we risk facing certain difficulties in helping our teams.

I used the quote from Benjamin Franklin at the beginning regarding things that are extremely hard because not only is it hard to know who we are, but the process to get there isn't all that easy either. There is an idea out there that says we never really know our own face, because we only see it in either photographs or in a mirror, but our significant other or family have full awareness of our true face, because they see it as it is from an outside perspective. The same can be said in regards to our personal position. We may have an idea of where we are and what we possess in terms of qualities, skills, and abilities, but we may not have the full picture.

Now you may be asking, "How can I really know where I am or my qualities?" or "Where do I go to get the full-picture?" Well, just as we discussed about our own face, we will need to depend on someone else to provide insight on our personal position. We can reflect or try and take a picture to get a good idea of where we are, and I highly suggest doing that, but I also believe in the importance of perspective.

Having someone we trust and respect give us an analysis of what they perceive to be our strengths, abilities, areas of opportunity, and overall character traits is great. But what can be more useful is having multiple people provide that type of assistance. Just as we may have a "good" or "bad" side of our face to take or not take pictures of, we have different areas of our personal position that we will need to be aware of in order to progress, and by having multiple "reviews" of our position, we can get a complete picture of those areas.

Let me stress this point: this is not an easy endeavor. We as humans are not keen on having the truth laid on us by others, let alone *asking* someone to do it to us. It can be difficult and stressful, but just as Mr. Franklin stated, knowing one's self is <u>hard</u>. But no one said being a good leader would be easy.

By having a trusted mentor, leader, colleague or friend provide us an honest review of what they perceive to be our strengths, skills, and areas of opportunity, it will provide us a better idea of our personal position. This is not to say you take every single thing they say to heart, but by understanding an outside perspective of what others understand of us, we can know how our team and the people we lead can see us and perceive us, and subsequently use that information to influence and engage with our team.

We all have areas that need attention and development, areas that we are proud of, and areas we depend on to succeed. Once we've identified these areas and have come to terms with them, then we don't have to worry about navigating through unchartered aspects of our self at times when our team needs us most.

That is the reason why it is so important to engage in self-analysis. If we can't take the time to obtain an honest and transparent view of ourselves, then how we can expect our team to do be open and honest when the time comes for us to analyze their positions and potential and make crucial decisions?

A number of years ago, I had a personal friend and a work colleague who knew of my career, experience, and character go through this exercise for me. They gave me an extensive list of what they thought were my strengths: patience, understanding, emotional intelligence and more. However, what proved to be more useful that knowing what I was good at was being told things that I needed to improve upon.

One of the perceptions they had of me was that I could come across as being indecisive, and essentially lacking confidence. Though I thought I always portrayed an air of confidence and consistency, they told me otherwise. After considering this, I came to the conclusion that the perception of indecisiveness was derived from me having a terrible habit of over analyzing information prior to making a decision and second-guessing myself once I did. What I came to understand was that my hesitance and fence sitting caused people on my team to not fully trust in my choices. They would go with it, but not as committed and completely as I would've expected. Basically, if I didn't fully believe in my own choices, than why should they?

By having a person or persons help me analyze my personal position, I understood that I needed to fix that perception of tentativeness. I began to work on trusting on my instincts, simplifying my information analyses, and standing by my decision in the face of outside criticism or challenges. As a result, my team began to have more confidence in me and could then focus more on their own responsibilities rather than spend time wondering if I was doing the right thing and making the right choices.

As I mentioned before, it is not easy to hear that people can clearly see our flaws, let alone flaws you did not even know you had. However, by becoming aware of them, we can work upon them and improve them. And with that transparency, we gain a level of respect from the people we are charged to lead.

The one thing I feel is detrimental to a team's trust in their leadership is when the leadership's integrity and honesty is put into question. As I stated earlier, no one is perfect, including us a leaders. To pretend that we are or that we have all the answers or even the old "do as I say, not as I do" mentality are not acceptable ways to lead.

Along those lines, there is something to be said aside from asking whether or not we are capable or have the right qualities to be a leader. And that is desire. Do we *want* to be a leader?

Often times when we consider what qualifies a person to be a leader we think about abilities or experience or education. Does this person have the right tools to lead? Have they had experience leading a team? But less often we ask if they have the heart to be a leader, and that is crucial.

After looking within and having our personal position and abilities audited, we must decide whether or not we have the desire and drive to be in that position. Not only because of the work involved, but the sacrifices the position could require us to make.

Our teams are like a car. Our team members are like the wheels, frame, and body of the car. They are what come together to fulfill the idea and complete the picture. The skills, training, and abilities we've obtained as leaders act like the engine components and drive train of that car. We serve to help guide and push the team in the right direction and with the right speed and power.

However, regardless of how great the car looks or how well it's built; or how efficient and oiled our engine and transmission are, they are all useless and motionless without one key component: fuel.

Without gasoline, diesel, or electricity, our car goes absolutely nowhere. The fuel is what sparks the entire engine, turns the belts and drives, and powers the car forward. When we speak about our teams and our leadership, passion and heart is what fuels the operation. If we try and lead a team without our urge to help our team attain its goals, it will be like driving a car on empty. That is why it is so crucial to ensure we have that fuel, that passion. Once we inject our heart and drive into the engine that is our experiences and abilities, it will then spread to the rest of the vehicle, charging every part that makes up the car making it go, go, go.

When we look at what drives us, what moves us as leaders, quality means a lot as well. Just as the fuel quality can affect our car's engine and system, our motivations and aspirations can have a lasting impact on our team's functionality as well.

If we take our team-as-a-car analogy a step further, imagine our crew as a high-end sports car. Streamlined frame, craftsmanship interior, supercharged motor, and all the bells and whistles you can imagine. Just like the individuals that make up our groups, it is top of the line. Knowing this, you wouldn't just go ahead and put it any gas in it, would you? In fact, if you read some car manuals of sports cars, they suggest you put in high-octane or premium fuel in order to maximize performance.

Now I am no mechanic, and maybe there is a conspiracy between auto manufacturers and the oil industry to get you to spend more money on gas, but I believe there is something to be said to when it comes to the fuel we use and its impact on our car's performance. I have a Ford Mustang, and as any car admirer, I try my best to keep the car running as well and as best as possible. With that, I have noticed a difference when I put it in regular gas compared to premium. I don't know what the exact science is behind it, but she always runs better when I put the premium gas in. Or maybe my Mustang is in on the conspiracy.

Regardless of the nuances, better fuel provides better performance. We see it with cars and we see it with nutrition. The better quality of the food, or fuel, the better we feel and run. So we must ask ourselves: What drives us to be leaders? What are our motivations and expectations? These are some key questions to ask ourselves to really determine if we are ready to lead, because these are the factors that are going to make up the fuel that will power our teams.

Ideal fuel for our leadership role needs to be one that ensures our team is at the forefront. If our motivation is for self-elevation, recognition, or promotion, than our gas has water in it. It will slow our car down or stall it all together. Corrupt or unclean fuel will sooner or later cause damage to the entire system.

With that said, if our motivations and aspirations for the team are for its ultimate success, regardless of how much or how little we are recognized as leaders, than we have premium, high-octane fuel in the tank. It will quietly and efficiently power our vehicles forward, helping the entire system work as intended.

As I stated earlier, our leadership is like the engine, the motor that drives the car. And as such, even though we are important to the function of the car, we are still, ultimately, under the hood. What needs to stand out and be seen are the pieces that make up the team, like the strong body, gleaming wheels, and impeccable interior. We need to make sure that we are in a position to ensure that the talents, skills, and work put in by our team members are what are put on display and on the forefront of our leadership work.

Between discovering our personal position and abilities and analyzing our motivations, we can start to build our leadership foundation. This is the only part of the SKIE idea that solely about us individually as leaders. We must look within to determine if we can lead. We can easily fool a person to think we are ready and convince others that we can be great leaders, but in the end the improper motivations, lack of desire, or unknowingness of our own self can ultimately lead us to fail our teams when it means the most.

Before taking the reigns of a leadership position, take the time to self-analyze and really get to know yourself and what makes you who you really are. By doing so, you will realize so much more about not only being a great leader, but about being something much more important: being a great person.

Chapter 2: Know

"To understand the heart and mind of a person, look not at what he has already achieved, but at what he aspires to."
-Kahlil Gibran

We have already discussed the importance of knowing our self, knowing the factors and tidbits that come together to form us as a whole. With that knowledge we can determine if we are ready to go and lead a team of people. But what about those people? What do we know (or not know) about them that can help (or hurt) or our aspirations to reach the destination we are heading to? Beyond that, what do we know (or not know) about that destination? Or the road to it? What do we know?

There are a series of questions commonly known as the 5 W's. They are: Who? What? Where? When? Why? They are mostly used in journalism and investigative practices to try and obtain basic information regarding a particular event or situation. However, we are going to use them in a slightly different manner. There are going to help us know more about our team and its overall purpose.

While all five questions are important for our use, we are going to focus primarily on the Who, What and Why. The reason being is that the When and Where can vary distinctly and can change as your team meets certain achievements and as they encounter new stages on their course.

So What? There are several What's we must ask about our team and ourselves. The first is to identify what is the purpose of the team? Is it to solve a problem? Develop a new idea? Coordinate an activity? Manage a project? Come up with a new donut flavor? Stop an alien invasion?

Regardless of what kind of team we are leading, it was formed to meet a certain goal or achievement. So as the leader of the team, it is up to us to determine and fully understand what the team has been brought together for. That can either be gleamed from either the authority that placed us in that position or, if we have decided to form the group ourselves, than we may have the purpose already in mind, we just need to ensure it's clear to the team and ultimately, us.

The reason this is so important is because knowing the what behind the formation of our crew will help us either compose the components of our team or determine what abilities, skills, and experience our team members will need to possess in order to fulfill the purpose.

It is just like painting a picture. If we know the scene or object we want to paint, then we'll have an idea of the colors we will need. Let's say we want to paint a daytime beach scene. We're going to have sand, the ocean, blue sky with some fluffy clouds, bright sun, perhaps a few seashells and maybe a pelican or two.

So now that we know what we are painting, we know that we will need some primarily colors like blue for the ocean, yellow for the sun, and white for the clouds in the sky. However, we are going to need some different colors for some other aspects of our beach scene. What if we decided to include a nice palm tree into our painting? We would need green for the leaves, right? Green is not a primary color, though. In order to get green we would need to mix blue and yellow together. And if we wanted a lighter shade, we would probably need to mix in some white to get the right green for those palm leaves.

It is the same with our teams. We may have members that are our primary colors. They have great communication, actionable skills, or a wealth of experience. They are easy to work with and could make up the core of our team. We know how and where to use them. Conversely, some primary colors are not as easy to incorporate into every painting.

Back to our beach masterpiece. We have bright colors like yellow and white. We mixed blue and yellow to get our green. Looks great. But what about black? In most basic paint sets it's a basic, primary color, but where do we incorporate it into our scene? Do we just leave it out?

We had mentioned we would like to include a couple pelicans into our artwork. Most pelicans I have seen are brown, but I've seen a couple with some shades of gray. Well in order to get gray we would have to take white and mix in a little black and, *voila*, we have our gray pelican. Yes, I have seen a number of episodes of *The Joy of Painting*. Thank you Bob Ross and your happy little trees.

We can have people on our team whose purpose and primary impact will not be as an individual contributor, but in addition to, or part of, another individual's contribution, or just as well, they can partner together cohesively and have significant input. They may have skills and talents that are unique, and rather than exclude them or marginalize them due to the distinctiveness of their specific tools, we can use them in conjunction with other components of our team and amplify them.

Cue the second important W: Who? Who are the members of the team? Who are these individuals that we've been tasked with bringing together to achieve the purpose we've previously identified? And what do we know about them and their experience that we can utilize in reaching our ultimate goal?

By making it a point to get to know our team members, we can accomplish two important tasks: We get to know the individuals that we are going to be working with on a more detailed level, helping build trust and cohesiveness; and we begin to know what their individual talents and abilities are, helping us become more aware of the tools and skills our team has at its disposal.

There is an interesting television show I enjoy watching on the Food Network called *Chopped*. For those of you who have never seen it, the premise of the show is that four chefs compete over 3 rounds of cooking in order to win the grand prize of $10,000 and the title of *Chopped Champion*. The twist to this competition is that in each round the chefs are presented with a basket of four mystery ingredients that are completely unknown to them, and they are charged with creating a unique dish using the four basket ingredients along with whatever ingredients that are available to them in the pantry. Each round is timed, and at the end of the allotted time they present their dishes to a panel of judges who decide which chef is "chopped". The rest move on to the next round and so on until one chef is left.

While it might sound like I am suggesting you put your team through a grueling cooking competition to determine who's your most valuable member, it is not; although it does sound like a heck of a good time.

I am fascinated on how these chefs can come up with delicious creations in only 30 minutes without knowing what ingredients they have to use until right before the round starts. It takes creativity, composure, and confidence to be able to execute under such pressure.

So these chefs can develop flavors and textures with unknown ingredients under strict time constraints with incredible results. Imagine what they could do if they had 60 or 90 minutes rather than 30? Or if they were made aware of the ingredients hours before they had to cook? What kind of meals could they prepare then?

It is the same with our people. If we make the effort to know them and know more about them, then we are like the *Chopped* chefs but with more time to prepare. Each person is like the basket of mystery ingredients. We really don't know what we have to work with until we open the basket up and discover what skills and talents they have. The sooner we do that, the more time we have to develop the routines and plans needed to execute on the team's purpose.

That leaves us with Why. Why are our team members here? What is just as important as the answer we get to this question is the actual asking of it to begin with. By asking this question, it allows our colleagues to know we care about what motivates them and what their goals are. When we allow them to share with us what they aspire to achieve, it provides them the knowledge that we are not solely interested in what their skills and experience are and what they bring to the group, but that we want to help them reach their personal goals as well. We will delve a little deeper into this in the following chapters.

Knowing this information regarding the Who, What, and Why of our team enables to build on our foundation of our team. By knowing the Who, we know our team and what they can capable of. By knowing the What, we know what the purpose of our team and what the expectations are, and by knowing the Why, we can know what motivates and drives the individual components of our crew.

Chapter 3: Invest

"Friend, there's no greater investment in life than in being a people builder. Relationships are more important than our accomplishments."
-Joel Osteen

Investing is a pretty straightforward concept: spend money on an item at a certain price now in the hopes that its value will increase over time, and thus produce a profit. There are seemingly normal things people invest in such as real estate, stocks, bonds, coins, and start-up businesses. Other things I've seen people invest in are stuff like artwork, comic books, and even wine of all things. Whatever it is, the purpose remains the same: put something in to get something profitable back out.

For the above examples of investing, we've been referring to using money as the form of currency that we would spend on our chosen investment. However, there is another form of currency that we can use with our team: time. I view time as a very valuable and powerful form of currency, one that can be used as wisely or as poorly as money.

A very distinct difference between money and time is that we cannot earn more time, and that makes time much more valuable. There is no part-time or moonlighting gig that we can take on that will pay us extra hours in the day or years in our life. There is no factory out there producing minutes or some lottery we can win that will give us years on our lives. We get 24 hours a day, 7 days a week, 365 days a year. That's our budget.

So how do we spend those precious seconds and minutes? I am a huge believer in work-life balance. This planet and its beauty have way too much to offer for us to just focus on work and work alone. We all have families, friends, hobbies, and dreams that deserve our time and attention. Are they getting it?

With my time spent as an Emergency Medical Technician I had the privilege of meeting countless people from all walks of life. From the less fortunate to the very blessed; from family matriarchs to new mothers; from heart-warming stories to tragic tales, I have experienced quite a bit. Part of that experience involved helping and spending time with the older members of our population.

Whenever I could, I enjoyed asking them questions. I did this for a number of reasons and one being that by engaging them in conversation usually helped with their situation. Sometimes the questions I asked about their past or family would take their mind off of their current pain or distract them a bit, providing a bit of alleviation.

The other reason I would ask is that I really enjoy learning about people, and I've learned that with all of our differences we have as people, we also have a lot in common. Similar joys, fears, dreams, and outlooks. They told me stories about their experiences and I heard them tell me about some terrific memories. They would tell me about people they met, events they saw, and things they got to see come and go. They would brag about their grand kids or great-grand kids and what they were doing now. But the one thing I can say for sure that I never heard them mention was that any of them looked back at their life and said, "I wish I spent more time at work".

Now let me say, many of them, especially veterans, were proud of the jobs they had or work they did. I met former teachers, police officers, nurses, bank tellers, factory workers and numerous other careers. They spoke to me about the effort they put in to start a family, buy a house, and the sacrifices made along the way to achieve those things. But not one regretted not being at the office more hours or wishing they had worked more evenings and weekends.

For me, my parents believed in working hard and working a lot. As a young kid my mom would do the housewife and mom work and then in the evening she would work in a factory. My father had his own contracting business and he put in A LOT of time. He loved his work and took pride in it. But he put in a lot of hours and did not always put spending time with the family first. We did not take a lot of family vacations and I spent most of my summers off as a teenager waking up early every day and going to work with my pops. He instilled in me a sturdy work ethic and I learned a lot from him, and I am grateful for it.

However, as I grew, and especially working in emergency services, my perspective changed some. I worked a lot, and as I started to respond to more motor vehicle accidents, cardiac arrests, strokes, and unresponsive patients I started to realize something I am sure we've all heard time and time again: that life is short. And that is truth, pure and simple.

As people and as leaders, we must take into account how we are spending, and investing, our time. For us individually, we spoke earlier about our motivations and how it's the fuel we are using to drive our team. Are we sure it is the premium fuel our teams need? What are we doing to ensure we are giving them our best? Part of that is to ensure we are in the right place in our hearts and mind to guide and direct our teams. Ask yourself, "Am I taking the time to make sure I'm ok?" "Am I in the right place to lead these people and work hard for them?" Let's take the time and invest some in ourselves, so we can invest some in them.

Investing time in our team can provide immeasurable returns throughout the length of our relationship with our team. When I say invest time, I am not talking about the time spent going over project details, progress reports, or any other job-related matter. I am talking about taking the time to find out information about our people and the answer to the Why question that we talked about in the previous chapter.

With all my teams, I made it a point to get to know my team members. It wasn't always easy, but like I said before, being a leader is not an easy endeavor. I would sit with them, one-on-one, and ask about their journey here, and where they saw themselves in the future. Sometimes I would get company lines like, "Oh, I want to be with this company for as long as possible" or "I want to know more about "x" or "y" position within the company".

These are not necessarily bad answers, and in some cases, I firmly believed that is what they were planning. Nevertheless, I wanted to know more. I wanted to know why there were here, what events transpired to get them here, what kind of decisions and choices did they make that led them here. I wanted to know more about the things they were good at, things they did outside of work or the group, things they did with their family or even what they wanted to be when they were younger. I wanted the whole basket of who they were, the complete picture. I wanted them to know I *cared* about them beyond what serviceable skills they possessed.

By investing my time in this manner, curious things took place. By showing that as their leader and colleague I cared about them as a person, they stopped looking at me as a manager or supervisor or boss, they saw me as a counterpart, someone who whole-heartedly wanted to help them not only in their current position, but to also help them as they continued on in their life and career. In return, I began to earn their respect.

As a leader, earning your team's respect is a high-level achievement. Because, if you act as just a manager or supervisor, they will fulfill tasks assigned to them because you've instructed them to do so and they will fear that if they fail, they will suffer a negative consequence to their job or position. They will see your authority as being *given* to you.

Gaining their respect, though, changes that dynamic. When you truly respect someone, you recognize his or her authority as being *earned,* instead of being just *given.* You earn your team's respect when you not only do the your individual work, but when you do your work with excellence and still take them time to work with them to make sure they have everything they need to excel as well. By going the extra mile and investing time in your team, you are ensuring profitable returns.

One person in my life that has always demonstrated this behavior to me, especially as a younger man, was Reverend Carlos E. Rivera. As the pastor of the church I grew up in, he always exuded true leadership. His job was to preach his sermons, help run the church, and be held accountable for the church's progress. But he did so much more.

My father was diagnosed with throat cancer when I was in the 4th grade. While undergoing radiation and other treatments, he couldn't work or even drive and my mother never learned how to drive to begin with. Thankfully for some family members' help, we never went without food or other necessities. But Rev. Rivera stands out.

I remember a time where I became sick at school and my nurse called my mother to let her know that I was going to be sent home. As I said, my mother couldn't drive, so who came to pick me up? Rev. Rivera. Without question or hesitation. When my father passed away a number of years ago, there weren't many people in the hospital with my mother, sister, and I, but Rev. Rivera was there. He showed care and compassion that went beyond his expected duties and responsibilities.

There are a number of more examples I can share of his leadership abilities, and maybe some out there would say that he was just doing his job, and maybe you're right. But his actions, demeanor, and *care* made an impact on my life and as I developed into a leader in the church and in my career, I took his lessons and actions as the example of what true leadership is and should be.

I am not saying that you have to be on-call for your team 24 hours a day, or show up to their family events. But what I am trying to get you to understand is how much we can positively impact our teams with the time and energy we invest in them. By showing we are more than simply managers or supervisors and that we genuinely care about them as human beings, we show them a higher level of commitment and demonstrate what we expect in return from them.

Doing this takes work, takes energy, and of course, takes time. But the results are worth it. The investment of time builds them up as people, and in the end, our job as leaders is much more than accomplishing a task or fulfilling a goal; we are meant to elevate and empower our people.

Chapter 4: Empower

"If your actions inspire others to dream more, learn more, do more and become more, you are a leader."
-John Quincy Adams

There is a simple concept that encapsulates what a leader's true purpose is: to empower others. We are leaders not so we can be on top of a pedestal, but that we become the pedestal so that our teams can be put on display. There will be moments we are in the spotlight or called to the forefront, but those are moments we can still use to empower our team and highlight what they have achieved and are still capable of.

For me, empowering your team is a continual process. The previous actions we've discussed in this SKIE Initiative are steps in completing the empowerment process. From preparing ourselves as leaders, to knowing our team and our goals, and to investing time and energy, these actions help us provide the vigor and spark to push our team members to new heights.

There are several things we can do as leaders to empower our teammates. In the previous chapters we talked about getting information about our people and understanding their drives and motivations. Here, we can take that information and put into action to help our colleagues progress in their lives and careers.

I had come into an organization once that emphasized customer service and delivering a great experience. The team had not had a consistent leader in a long time and the last director they had was not focused on their success, rather had focused more on her rise up the corporate ladder. However, the assistant director had done an incredible job holding the team together and had taken it upon herself to ensure that they maintained their expected level of success. I was intrigued about this dynamic and immediately got to work analyzing how I could help, getting to know the team and their goals, and began investing my time and energy to elevate them and their performance.

The one curious fact I learned is that the assistant director, we'll name her Jessica, had been with the company for over 11 years, and had been in the assistant director position for the past six. When I sat down with her to go over her experience and her career goals, I had to ask why she never had even attempted to interview for the director position, seeing as there had been so many opportunities to do so. Jessica's response: "I don't think I have what it takes."

That blew me away. To me it was as clear as day that this person had every quality to lead this team. More than that, Jessica had the *heart* to be a wonderful leader. She showed commitment, care, and exemplified the work ethic needed to impact her team. She knew all the individual people who made up the crew, their strengths, where they could improve, and showed empathy when required and proved to be an irreplaceable resource for them.

It was evident that while Jessica possessed the tools, abilities, and passion it took to lead the group and lead them well, the one thing that was missing was the encouragement and empowerment needed for her to take that next step. So I made it a priority to ensure that she, along with the rest of the crew, was made aware of all the opportunities that they were more than capable of taking advantage of.

First, I had to make sure she wanted the role of director. Desire is an underrated aspect of making career choices. Many people feel obligated to take a promotion or make a change out of societal expectations or other pressures. We feel a promotion is the only way we can show we are succeeding, or validate our work, or that believing a salary increase is the only way of showing we are progressing. Without desire, without passion, these changes cannot have the fulfilling sensation we expect. So I needed to know if Jessica really wanted that challenge.

So during one our conversations she mentioned she always wanted to be the director. That she felt she could handle the responsibility, and more importantly, she wanted it. She also told me something that I found interesting: Many people told her that she should be the director, but no one told her that she *could*. Not *could* in the sense she was qualified, but in the sense that she really could *excel* at the role, that she had what it takes to succeed. That she owned the ability and heart to be the leader the team needed.

After understanding her aspirations, and explaining to her she could be a dynamic and engaging leader, I began to work with her to understand the other aspects of the role, but more importantly, how to continue to empower her team in their respective roles to help uplift them and the entire team as a single unit.

With the time and energy invested, and working together, today she is the director for her team and is excelling. Not only did this type of leadership help a person take another step in their career, but by implementing the same power and care into the rest of the team, they are all aware of what they are capable of and have received the encouragement to pursue their goals.

I don't share this story as a way to promote my abilities, or myself, but to demonstrate how empowering our people and focusing our energy on our teammates, we can help them rise up and take on new challenges and have new experiences. In the end, if I have made a positive impact on their lives, then I have achieved success.

As individuals, the people we come into contact with, let alone have the opportunity to work along side of, are all potential opportunities to make a positive impact in their lives. As leaders, we must take advantage of those opportunities, especially with the people that are on our teams and in our lives.

As the author and speaker Simon Sinek said:

"Most people think leadership is about being in charge. Most people think leadership is about having all the answers and being the most intelligent person or the most qualified person in the room. The irony is that it is the complete opposite. Leadership is about empowering others to achieve things they did not think possible. Leadership is about pointing in the direction, articulating a vision of the world that does not yet exist. Then asking help from others to insure that vision happens."

Last Thoughts

"If there is anything I would like to be remembered for it is that I helped people understand that leadership is helping other people grow and succeed. To repeat myself, leadership is not just about you. It's about them"
-Jack Welch

One of the things that inspire me and help me be a leader is the fact that counter to popular belief; leading is about serving, not taking. True leadership is selfless, not selfish, expelling positive energy, not draining it from others; it's about investing time and not withdrawing from those we lead.

My ultimate goal for this SKIE initiative is that those of you who are reading this become motivated to improve upon your relationships with your teams. That you take the time to evaluate your personal position and understand the areas that you can work on. That you really get to know your people and the goals ahead of you and them, and that you invest the time and energy in your team to ensure they have all the assets and means they need to succeed. Lastly, empower your team. Encourage them to chase their dreams regardless of what they may be, and inspire them to be the best they can be. And in doing so, you will discover a sense of accomplishment that cannot be matched.

Thank you for taking the time to read this work and for supporting this man's journey in life. Be well. Experience focusing

[End]